30 1
Hawaiian Manifestation Plan

By Jill Gregory

Section1 Jill's Coaching

Section 2 Law of the Universe

Section 3 Huna 1

30 Day Hawaiian Manifestation plan (to get anything & everything you've ever wanted) 🌈🦄⛟

COPYRIGHT

First published February 2024

Copyright © Protect my work

All rights reserved. No part of this publication may be reproduced, stored in a retrieval system or transmitted in any form or by any means without the prior permission in writing of the author.

Contents

Introduction: 7

Day 1...9

  Day 1: what do you want/not want in and for your life?? 10

Day 2... 18

  Day 2 Learning your 6 human needs: 19

Day 3... 22

  Day 3: Write a letter.. 23

Day 4... 27

  Day 4: Make a plan... 28

Day 5... 30

  Day 5: Learn how to Daydream/Visualise - to be done every day. 31

Day 6... 34

  Day 6: Dream Circle/Vision board............................. 35

Day 7... 38

  Day 7: Remove your blocks extremely important to your manifestation. 39

Day 8... 42

  Day 8: Beliefs and values. 43

Day 9... 46

  Day 9: Your experiences. 47

Day 10 49

Day 10: Negative emotions and worry 50

Day 11 ....**52**

Day 11: How your emotions affect you 51% rule..... 53

Day 12 ....**55**

Day 12: Vibes, Energy. 56

Day 13 ....**58**

Day 13: Enjoy yourself... 59

Day 14 ....**61**

Day 14: Dance and flow with the universe/Hula/Lomi Lomi.. 62

Day 15 ....**65**

Day 15: laugh/comedy movies. 66

Day 16 ....**68**

Day 16: Affirmations/Learn to write your own affirmations... 69

Day 17 ....**72**

Day 17: Using your senses to manifest......................... 73

Day 18 ....**75**

Day 18: The Law of attraction, a Universal law 76

Day 19 ....**79**

Day 19: Law of Assumption.. 80

Day 20 ....**82**

Day 20: Who are your Role models/Idols?................... 83

Day 21 ....**85**

Day 21: Love yourself/Increase your self esteem and your uniqueness & smile. 86

Day 22 .... **88**

Day 22: Gratitude/Gratitude journal to do every day
....89

Day 23 .... **91**

7 Huna Principles: 91

Day 23: . IKE: The world is what you think it is. 92

Day 24 .... **94**

Day 24: KALA: There are no limits ... Freedom 95

Day 25 .... **97**

Day 25: MAKIA: Energy flows where attention goes.
....98

Day 26 .... **100**

Day 26: MANAWA: Now is the moment of power... 101

Day 27 .... **103**

Day 27: ALOHA: To love is to be happy with............. 104

Day 28 .... **106**

Day 28: MANA: All power comes from within.......... 107

Day 29 .... **109**

Day 29: PONO: Effectiveness is the measure of truth.
.... 110

Day 30 .... **112**

Day 30: How far have you come on your journey and
do you need to add any more milestones?................. 113

Life is but a dream……..

So dream the life you want into reality.

30 Day Hawaiian manifestation plan

The guaranteed plan to manifest the life you have only ever dreamed of.

Introduction:

I've been interested in Metaphysical subjects for as long as I can remember. As is explained in chapter 29 of this book, the Huna principle PONO Effectiveness is the measure of truth. What I have been doing all my life is learning as much as possible and making sense of, and testing the effectiveness of all I have learnt over the years; putting it together and making it into a full picture that makes perfect sense to me.

I started to read Metaphysical books by the late great Gill Edwards, who I met at her home in the Lake District , and got to do a workshop course with her. Reading Gill Edwards books then lead me onto books by the amazing Serge Kahili King, my Huna teacher and mentor. I went on to learn Tarot and all things magical and natural. I learnt a bit of healing and meditating along the way.

Amidst a few mundane jobs and the joyous arrival of my son, I made a life-altering decision to work from home, enabling me to be present for my child while pursuing Metaphysical Life Coaching. That taught me a lot about how to help people move ahead with their goals in life and, in turn, move ahead with my goals in my own life. I also realised that I had to conquer a major block in my life to move ahead with my own life. I realised I had a social phobia that I had to get over or I would never be able to achieve my goal of becoming a Life Coach. I did this using any method I could (PONO again). I tried hypnotherapy, healing of various types and speaking to my doctor. Thanks to all of these methods combined I managed to control my fear up to about

95% cured. I am still working on that last 5% but I suppose an element of fear is only human.

Despite the fact that I was learning Metaphysical Life Coaching, I felt there was something missing in the way things were put across. I felt I needed to do it and teach it my way.

I then decided I would like to learn hypnotherapy. Which I did and started my own practice in 2014. Hypnotherapy is a great way of releasing things that are unconsciously running your life. Your life is running on autopilot, until you decide to change something consciously. It's a great way to release parts of your subconscious that are a block and will hold you back from moving forward with many parts of your life.

In the meantime I was also fascinated by the new fascination of the Law of Attraction and how it affects your life for the better. After reading many authors, including, Rhonda Byrne, Ester and Gerry Hicks, Deepak Chopra, etc. I found that even all those books didn't feel 100% right to me. I knew that I needed to work out what I felt works. That, in turn, has led to my work the '30 Day Hawaiian Manifestation plan'.

This plan gives you a 30 day/step programme to move you into the perfect life you have always dreamed of. Please join me in creating this life now.

Day 1

Day 1: what do you want/not want in and for your life??

You have to decide what you want to be able to get it. Knowing what you don't want in life can also be positive, it helps you to know what you DO want.

Make a definite list of what you would like to bring into your life. A goal, a material possession, people, a relationship etc. Start with what you DON'T want. Make an opposites list.

The Universe will respond if you have made a definite decision as to what you want. Make a list of what you want but don't forget to be very specific with the details. Don't manifest a new house with horrible neighbours for example. The specifics are very important.

Here is an exercise to look at the various life areas when you are listing what you want. Fill in the questions. They will help you to write your 'future self' letter later. Using but not limited to these life areas:

Health:

Do you have any physical goals you would like to achieve?

What would your ideal weight be?

What size clothes would you like to fit into?

Would you like to follow a specific lifestyle diet or eat more organic food?

Would you like to learn yoga/climb a mountain, cycle through the South of France? Climb volcanos in Hawaii or swim in the sea?

Go on a retreat?

Family:

Create your own family?

Improve relations with family members?

Do a family tree?

Help family members?

Friends:

Make new friends?

Spend more time with friends?

Holidays with friends?

Help friends?

Money:

How much money would you like to have in the next 5 –10 years?

How much passive income would you like?

Would you like to look into investing money on the stock market etc?

Would you like to invest in property?

How much money would you need to retire?

How much disposable income would you like when you retire?

How much money would you like each year for travelling and holidays?

What would you like your net worth to be?

Which property would you want to own? Make plans. Seriously look into it. Look on YouTube for luxury properties in places you would like to stay/live.

Career:

Who would you like to work for?

Would you like to work for yourself/Have your own business?

Would you like to learn something new to start a new career?

What age would you like to retire?

Where would you like to work? London, New York Paris or from home?

How much do you want to work?

Do you not want to work at all?

Do you want to start your own charity and run that or get someone else to run it?

Do you like to work alone or with a team of people?

Is there anything you could be teaching other people or that you would like to teach other people?

Where would your working environment be? Outside or in a nice office?

Self-development:

If you were fearless what would you do?

What skills do you need or want?

Do you want to have achieved something in the next 5-10 years?

Do you want to learn a language?

Would you do public speaking on a subject that you know a lot about?

Is there anything you would like to work on in your life that you can look into things like therapy, Hypnotherapy, Life Coaching, Healing, even seeing a doctor to look into any health problems etc?

Spiritual:

Is there a Spiritual retreat that you would like to attend?

Is there a Spiritual development group you would like to join?

Do you want to do more meditation?

Spend time by a beach or a peaceful area?

Write more?

Partner:

What would your ideal partner be like?

Write down a list of qualities of your perfect partner.

Do you want to be married or live with a partner?

Would you like to spend a lot of time with your partner?

What things would you like to do with your partner?

Do you like a lot of intimacy?

Would you like to have children or more children?

What sort of a partner would you be?

Now using the above exercise. Write down for each life area, a list of everything you would like in each life area. It will also give you an idea of where you are in life at the moment. Find at least 3 life areas that you would like to work on and then do some brainstorming on those life areas and make sure you are very specific on each subject. Do not leave anything out as you manifest what you think about. You don't have to limit yourself to 3 but maybe concentrate on 3 and move on to more later.

Imagine that each life area was a 10. Rate each life area as it is at the moment. For example if Health is a 5 imagine what you would have to do to bring this life area up to a 10. Do the same for each life area.

Now do a brainstorming session on each life area you would like to work on. Also when you do this the sky is the limit. Do not limit yourself by resources, as you can manifest whatever you would like or need. But also realise that if your dream does not feel achievable deep down and you don't believe its achievable then it will be very hard to manifest it in one go. You may have to slowly but surely work up to the thing amount you would like. For example, if you would like to manifest a million but deep down you think fifty thousand is achievable then start with fifty thousand and work up to the amount you would really like and you'll begin to feel comfortable with larger amounts.

Imagine that you were given a lamp with your very own genie in it. When you rub the lamp and the genie pops out. You are not only limited to 3 wishes – you can ask as many as you would like. Write down the perfect scenario for each life area to bring that life area up to a 10. Remember to be specific! You will hear that a lot in this book. If you want a partner be very specific about the partner you would like to manifest. List every quality that you would like in that person. If you want a dream house, be very specific about the type of house you would like. How many rooms. How many bedrooms, bathrooms, cinema room etc. Make sure to mention how much land you would like, if you would like a pool or a jacuzzi or tennis court etc. Say where you would like your house or houses to be. Which country and area. If you would like a new car/cars then you need to list the type of car you would like or how many cars/garages. If you want pets, list down how many and which type of pets you would like. This is very important when doing this brainstorming session.

These life areas can give you an idea of what you might want to work on in your life and what might be missing in your life. The 6 human needs, in the next chapter may show you more of what you want or need and what may be missing in your life for your happiness.

When you think about money don't limit yourself to how much you have at the moment. Realise that you can manifest as much as you feel you would like using the methods in this book.

If you want to manifest money imagine money as the amount of water in the sea. There is unlimited amounts of water and unlimited amounts of money. Just reach out and take whatever you need or want. Or imagine that when you go to a cash machine that you can take out unlimited amounts of money.

If you are talking about health mention what you are doing for your body/health to keep it fit and healthy or improve your health.

If you have chosen to mention and work on the spiritual side of your life then be very specific about what you are doing – specify if it's meditation or yoga or a specific spiritual pursuit.

If you are changing your career to a career path that you will enjoy more, be very specific about the career you would like to do. How you would dress? Where the work premises would be? What you would be doing on a daily basis?

If you have chosen to work on your personal development then list the courses you would like to do and/reading that you would like to do etc.

Friends and Family:

Be very specific about your Friends and Family goals.

How many friends you would like. How large you would like your family to be. If you would like to get on better with your family, descibe how you would have done this.

Always remember that when you are listing in these life areas that you are writing them in the present tense and in positive language.

Complete this exercise before moving onto day 2.

Day 2

Day 2 Learning your 6 human needs:

Getting your human needs balanced is extremely important for your happiness in Life. Make sure you're getting your human needs met and including them in your goals and life plan.

The 6 human needs are:

Stability: Knowing you have a stable life/income. Everybody needs some stability in their lives. Its not to say you don't want any excitement, but for you to feel happy you need a bit of stability in your life. A place to come home to. A base. Even if you travel a lot it is always nice to have somewhere to come home to. Without this stability we would feel very unsettled and it would take away from our happiness in life.

Variety: change and new stimuli. If you find yourself always living a 9 to 5 life, where you are doing the same thing every day you will soon become depressed as everyone needs a bit of variety in their lives. Even if the variety means a yearly holiday, we all need something different to look forward to.

Significance: Feeling special and unique.

To be happy in life you need to feel you are significant and have made a good contribution to the world or at least people around you. To feel significant we need to feel like we are important to people in our lives, whether it is our children, partners, family or friends. We also need to feel like we are different from other people. We need to feel like we are independent. Unfortunately too much significance and independence can make us feel disconnected from others.

Love and Connection: feeling you've connected with someone and you are loved. Family, friends and relationships. You also need people in your life who love or at least like your company. Being alone can be ok for a while but you will soon feel lonely and it will make you very unhappy. Connection is also feeling part of a community.

Growth: Learning and expanding your knowledge. This need is about learning and growing. It makes you happy to know that you are always learning new things, and exploring the world and learning about new subjects.

Contribution: service and support to others. Support for a community. Feeling like we are giving what we can to whoever we can, and giving of your free time to people or charities.

Exercise:

Have a look at your life at the moment and see if you have all your basic human needs in your life met? Are the ones that need to be balanced, balanced?

Finish this exercise before moving on to day 3.

Day 3

Day 3: Write a letter

Write a letter from your future self. Write a letter to yourself from your future self or write it to someone you know, a family member, if you would prefer to do that. Date the letter with a future date. For example a year or 5 years from now.

Here is the exercise:

1. Take a piece of nice writing paper.

2. Start to compose your letter on this nice writing paper.

3. Date the letter in the future. For example if you would like to achieve your goal in a years time, date your letter for exactly a years time.

If you would like to achieve your dream/goal in 2 years time, write the date on the top of your letter as exactly 2 years from now.

4. Start writing your letter. Start by using the sentence: "It is now (1/2 years time for example) I am now extremely happy and fulfilled, as I am......... "

5. Explain exactly how your life is wonderful now.

6. Explain how great you are feeling.

7. Explain where you are living/city/town, what sort of home you have, what car you are driving, what pets you have etc.

8. What you are doing for a living.

9. Whether you have a partner/children.

10. Anything else you would like to add about your wonderful life you are living.

Give yourself a definite date to achieve your dreams/timeline.

Very important. If you say you are going to do something in the future it will always stay in the future.

So when you are setting goals you need to give the goal a definite date.

A tip that I have learnt lately is to realise that time is running out to achieve your dream. Realise that you have to go after your dream with such passion like you would go after a holiday you want/a concert you want to see/ a theatre production you want to see. Airplanes and concerts don't wait for you, you have to be ready for them. Make sure the tickets are sorted, suitcases packed, everything is ready for your dream. If you want to move house then start packing you current house up, even if you don't have it yet. That should be your first task. Then the Universe will start conspiring to bring your new home to you.

Live your life like you already have achieved your goal. If you want a new partner then sleep on one side of your bed. Make room in your closet for your partners clothes. If you want a new job imagine you already have the job. Dress the way you would dress if you have the job. Set your alarm at the time you would get up for your new job. Imagine waking up in the house you would like to live in and in the Country/City/town you would like to live in.

Don't forget to include your 6 human needs in your future letter. If you haven't covered your 6 human needs it takes away in the long run from your enjoyment of your newly created life.

Get a diary and map out the time you will do every step of your plan and goal, on day 4.

Write a list of the reasons you must achieve your dreams and goals by the certain date that you want to achieve your goals by. Your list may seem a bit negative but its a bit like a kick on the butt to do it.

It could be things like you would like to achieve a certain thing before you become a certain age. It can be before your children or your other family members, parents etc. are a certain age.

It can be to get away from the neighbourhood you are in. It can be to move to another country by a certain time. It can be for medical reasons or just to be able to help yourself and others.

Day 4

Day 4: Make a plan

Weekly milestones/achievements/ reward yourself.

Break your goals down into small milestones. Once you have decided on your big goals, break them down into smaller milestones. Write down the milestones for every week. Give yourself an award when you achieve your milestones. With the weekly milestones just give yourself a small reward and with your larger goals give yourself a larger reward. Even a small step in the right direction will be a big step towards your dream.

Now would a good time to get that diary I mentioned on day 3. Then go ahead and put those goals and dates that would like to achieve them in your diary. Take it as a step by step process. When you achieve your first step and then the next one it builds your confidence and in turn helps you to BELIEVE that your next steps are achievable and builds your confidence and your confidence and your vibrations rise, which in turn helps you manifest those all important goals.

Probably best to get a two year diary if you are going to achieve your goal in a year's time. Then you can put your completion date in for your goal.

Rewards don't have to be expensive presents. Just make sure you give yourself something you enjoy. You could do a massage swap with a friend. Take time out for a day at the beach or go shopping with a friend. Read a book. Have a tarot reading . Go for a nice spa day or swim. There are lots of things you can do to take some time out just for you.

Little milestones will add up to big parts of our goals. Even if its as simple as just getting some copier paper for your printer. Anything that would help.

Day 5

Day 5: Learn how to Daydream/Visualise

- to be done every day.

Spend some time during the day thinking that you do ALREADY have what you want in your life. Read that again…..What you already have. I find the best time of the day to do this is in the first part of the morning. So you can start off by manifesting your day ahead. Day dream as to how you would like your day ahead to look. It should become a very important part of your daily routine. The more that you see things in your day manifesting, the more you realise that you are able to manifest.

Think that you already have what you want in life. Use all your senses to do this activity.

Relax. Maybe lie down on your coach or somewhere that is comfortable and nice: a beach, a lovely bed, a warm conservatory, by a pool etc. Preferably get yourself a manifestation chair.

Dream about what you want in life. When you do this, use your senses. Imagine how you would feel if your dream came true. Important - you need to believe it to make it believable. Imagine the sensations. How happy, excited and wonderful you would feel. Imagine what you would see. Imagine what you would smell. If you are dreaming about a country imagine the warmth of the sun or the cool breeze or the biting icy cold of a cold country. If you want a new car imagine that you are sitting in the front seat of the car. Imagine what it would look like. Imagine how the car would smell. Imagine the sound of the car and the powerful turbo boost or smoothness of a large car. Imagine where you are driving. Imagine the terrain and scenery around you.

Do this as often as possible. Make daydreaming a daily habit.

Visualise how you would like certain scenarios to go in your life. If you would like to manifest a certain amount of money then visualise that amount of money in your bank account.

Imagine all the things you can buy with your money. Places you can go to. Holidays you can go on. Imagine people you could help as contributing is so important. It's a very important energy exchange. If you take your car in to be fixed, imagine it going well. If there is a car you would like, imagine yourself driving it and having fun. Visualising is so important. And visualising with feeling. It will not work unless you add feeling to it and believe it. How would you feel if you had that money, car, house etc?

But whatever you do don't feel desperate about what you want as then you will consequently push away your manifestation. Just believe you already have it and be a gracious receiver.

Day 6

Day 6: Dream Circle/Vision board

Once you have your exact ideas of what you want in your life, you can create a dream circle/vision board.

The vision board/dream circle can either be pictures that you cut out of magazines. You can use pictures that you print out on your printer,

OR it can be an electronic slide show. This can be created on your computer or laptop or on your smart phone. It can be simply done on your gallery of photos:

1. Create a folder in your photo gallery.

2. Name it. Maybe call it 'Vision board'.

3. Then use the option on your gallery to create a slide show.

Watch this slide show every morning. Preferably when you first wake up. This time in the morning is the time when your subconscious is open to new suggestions and in the mode to receive new suggestions.

If your vision board is a practical vision board or dream circle then place it on your fridge or on a cork board or anywhere in your house that you will see it and give lots of energy to it. Do not focus and obsesses over it too much but just let it go. Like a letter you send in the post, just trust that it will get to the destination and be received and worked on. Just trust and let go.

You will find very soon that either slowly and surely, or even surprisingly fast, these goals and dreams will start coming to you.

If money is what you would like to manifest, then either put some money up where you can see it or write yourself a cheque for that amount that you would like or print out your bank account statement and put the total as what you would like it to be. But it must believable to you. I know there are various websites that you can use to print out manifesting cheques that are blank that you can fill in the amount that you would like to manifest. Start small and move up bit by bit.

You can also place this printed out and filled in cheque on the ceiling above your bed so that you can look at it often and manifest the amount you would like faster.

Once you have made your dream circle or vision board or electronic vision board then let it go and don't hold onto your manifestation too tightly. Trust that the Universe will bring it to you. Like a letter that you post and trust that it will get to the destination.

Day 7

Day 7: Remove your blocks extremely important to your manifestation.

There are various way that people can remove mental blocks in their lives that are stopping them from manifesting certain things in their lives, especially money and love.

Nobody is perfect and none of us have come out of our childhoods unscathed. That doesn't mean that our childhoods or parents/carers were bad but we all get influenced greatly by our childhoods. We take on beliefs and wounds. Some that are ours too but some that are not. We may have been spoilt in our childhood which will make us feel entitled and then if we don't get what we want as fast as we would like it we get very upset and feel that we are hard done by.

Its not just our childhoods that can influence us but various other parts of our lives, partners, religion, relationships, culture, schools etc. I will cover this in another section.

The wounds from your past can be very large wounds and then we believe the world to be a very unfriendly and hostile place. We lose trust.

All of these past wounds, good or bad, need to be shifted to be able to give you as clean a slate as possible to manifest your dreams.

There are many different ways that blocks can be removed from your life. Some of these methods being:

- Talking to your GP to get help with any anxiety/depression that could be causing you to neglect yourself and your future.

- Getting any therapy, such as talking therapy, hypnotherapy, CBT, EMDR therapy for stuck trauma, etc.

- Healing

- Ho'oponopono….. Ho'oponopono is an ancient Hawaiian meditation to improve relationships by forgiveness and cutting aka chords.

- Acupuncture/Acupressure

- A retreat

- Rehab if necessary for various blocks.

- EFT

- Dynamind technique Is an Hawaiian method to help with various blocks. It is very similar to EFT. Created by Serge Kahili King.

- Meditation exercises to feel better about situations.

Having blocks could be a reason why you can only go so far with your goals in life. Removing those blocks will clear the way for all the abundance, relationships etc that you would like in your life.

Exercise:

Honestly assess your past wounds that you feel need working on and add them to your goals and milestones.

Day 8

Day 8: Beliefs and values.

Beliefs are very important in the manifestation process. More important than you realise. If you have been trying to manifest your desired outcome/money/house etc and you find you keep what you may think is 'failing' you, most probably have inner beliefs that are keeping you from manifesting. It is your subconscious that is blocking your dreams. Your subconscious is not trying to sabotage you but thinks it is protecting you from things that may have hurt you in the past. Its called Fight, flight, freeze or fawn response. One of the main ways to heal this subconscious mind program that is running is firstly by acknowledging it is happening. Acknowledging that you have this problem is very powerful - by first bringing it to the surface of your mind and then it will either automatically disintegrate or you will have to use some hypnosis to clear it deep from your subconscious mind. For example if your parents told you 'Money is the root of all evil'. that may stick in your subconscious mind and your subconscious will try and stop you from accumulating money so that you will be saved from that evil coming into your life. You will have to clear that belief out of your system to be able to make money.

There are many other statements about money which can be very damaging and stick in your subconscious mind.

Your parents/partners/religion. How your subconscious has run your life, when you are running on autopilot & you are not purposely directing your own life movie.

Beliefs in life come from many places. As you grow up you take on many different belief systems and values. Eventually we will create our own values based solely on what is important to us.

Sometimes beliefs are so deep in our subconscious that we will need something like hypnotherapy to change our deep seated patterns and automatic thoughts. Unless we make a conscious effort to control our thoughts, our subconscious will control a lot of what we think and do in life.

Making thoughts conscious and bringing them into the light of day will help to heal those beliefs and help us to realise that they were ruling our lives without us even knowing.

Exercise:

1. Meditate and write down any beliefs about the various life areas that you can think of that were passed on to you by your parents, community, school, religion, partners, work etc. For example 'Money doesn't grow on trees', 'Money is the root of all evil' etc.

2. Look at these various beliefs and acknowledge how they have influenced your life at present.

3. Create new beliefs. Write them down as the opposite of what you believe at the moment, if the current belief doesn't serve you and isn't positive.

Day 9

Day 9: Your experiences.

How what you have been through influences your life. You can use meditations to help you to heal negative experiences, especially if the negative experiences have caused a block in your subconscious preventing you from moving ahead with your life. Once again, hypnosis can be used to help you shift these blocks out of your system.

We have all been through many and different experiences in our lives. Our life experiences create our belief system in life too.

Experiences in life are like layers of an onion. They overlap, one on top of the other. So sometimes we have to heal them one at a time too. Get help for any experiences that you feel have left you feeling scared or scarred. These need to be dealt with first. Don't leave it too long as these experiences can produce fears and subconscious blocks that are stopping you from manifesting the life of your dreams.

Get free so you can write a new life story and run your own life.

Exercise:

How have your experiences in life influenced your beliefs and values and mind set? Realise you can change your mind set about the way these have affected you.

Day 10

Day 10: Negative emotions and worry

Negative emotions and worry do not get you anywhere in life and create negative manifestations. Worrying is manifesting what you do not want. The more you let your mind focus on the negative the more we push away our dreams. Worry is just asking the Universe for what we do not want.

Feeling guilty or having negative emotions or worry will always bring about negative manifestations.

Check in on yourself every few minutes. Check how you are feeling. Remember how important feelings are to manifestation.

Exercise:

Make a list of negative emotions that you feel on a regular basis. Look at things that need to be dealt with and see if you are overthinking sometimes. We see situations sometimes in a non-realistic way. Look at the whole situation and see if the way you are feeling is relevant or a fact. If not it is just an emotion and if you look at the situation and see you are worrying and it doesn't relate to a fact then we are worrying just for the sake of torturing ourselves.

If you feel you can't shake a certain feeling I would suggest maybe seeing someone who you feel comfortable with to help you with that negative emotion. A person of your choice. Professional or otherwise. Don't keep negative emotions buried deep inside. Not only is it not good for manifesting but its not good for your physical health. Disease stands for Dis-ease; when you are not feeling at ease. Emotions are very much linked to your health. There is a lot of wonderful information about this in Louise Hays book 'You can heal your life'.

1. Every day, count how many times you have negative emotions or say negative words. You'll be surprised how many times you do.

2. Go a whole week without complaining and see how your life changes for the better.

Day 11

Day 11: How your emotions affect you 51% rule

Energy/thoughts and emotions are like a magnet.

Realise that you are blocking your manifestation if you are not allowing yourself to feel on top of the world.

Blah feelings bring blah manifestations. Great feelings bring great manifestations. Bad feelings bring bad manifestations.

Sometimes faking it until you make it is the best thing to do for your moods and confidence. Even smiling can bring good feeling hormones to the surface. Smile with your eyes.

Use the 51% rule. Most people cannot always be in a good mood all of the time, some can but most can't. We are all human but check in on yourself, as I've mentioned a few times before, and make sure you tip the scale of good feeling during the day to at least 51%. On a bad day just get yourself feeling good for 51% of your day and you will be well on the way to manifesting a good rest of your day and further.

Another good way to help your emotions is to make sure that most of the time you stay in the present moment, and enjoy the present moment to the fullest. When you're worrying, ask yourself if you are in the present moment?

Exercise:

Check in on yourself every few minutes or so and see how you are feeling. Negative or positive.

Day 12

Day 12: Vibes, Energy.

This comes first in manifesting . You can give out your own vibes and absorb the vibes of the people around you. Your family, friends and co-workers and even people walking down the street. So always be aware of and protect your energy.

If you feel yourself getting down, then think of a thought of something or someone who brings you a very good memory and feeling and use this to change your vibe.

Another way of doing it is to see if you are in the moment. Ask yourself if you are you in the present moment. Asking this question if extremely powerful. It will not be your body answering this question but your soul. Your soul will bring you right back into the present moment. After a while of asking you will feel a blissful feeling and then hold on to that feeling of being in the present moment. You will manifest much quicker being in the present blissful feeling moment.

Vibes can also be used to see how you feel about a situation/person/place etc. Your vibes are also your instinct/intuition. If something doesn't feel right, it usually isn't. Be around people who give off good vibes.

Also, if you get your vibes aligned with what you would like to manifest, then your manifestation cannot help but be in your life. You need to be on the same vibration as your manifestation.

Exercise:

Experiment with feeling the energy of people and places. Experiment with your instincts and intuition. In every situation see what your instincts are telling you about people and situations.

Day 13

Day 13: Enjoy yourself

Make your life fun. You have one life to live as YOU. Make sure every day you do something you love and enjoy. Remember that life is short.

Exercise:

1. Make sure every day you do something you enjoy doing. It will help to brighten your mood and help you raise your vibes for the day. Schedule it into your day, so that you don't forget to include it in your routine. It can be something small but don't forget to do it. Maybe a walk in nature, a swim, a chat with a friend, watch your favourite programme, listen to your favourite music, read a book or some of a book etc.

2. On the weekends plan something fun and nice to do with family or friends or both.

Don't work 24/7. Do work that you enjoy and make sure you have enough time off for yourself and your interests.

Get a hobby that you enjoy: dancing, a spiritual pursuit, art, crafts, singing, car shows etc.

Make time for holidays and weekends away. Every now and again plan a nice long weekend somewhere, even just to visit and stay with friends. Make sure you put money aside for a lovely holiday. Give yourself something special to look forward to.

Day 14

Day 14: Dance and flow with the universe/Hula/Lomi Lomi

To go with the flow of the Universe is the best way to always be. Moving your body, your muscles in a way that makes you feel the flow of the Universe is so important. It can be any sort of dancing.

There are many videos on YouTube about learning how to do Hula dancing or you can join a class or learn on the beautiful islands of Hawaii itself.

Just keeping your body moving will do you the world of good. Hawaiian dance (Hula) and massage (Lomi Lomi) were especially created to keep the body in the flow of the Universe. Hula is a beautiful fluid motion. It is enjoyable to watch and do. Lomi Lomi is the most flowing of all of the massages. The masseur uses their whole body, almost in a dance to create a flowing movement to keep the body flowing. They will use their elbows and whole body to put the flow of the Universe back into your body. Some people have found a lymphatic massage helps with the flow of things in the physical body. Then if your physical body is flowing then your mind will be flowing too.

Go with the flow of life. Try not to stress about every change or surprise. You find people who live a long time go with the flow of life. Chill out as much as possible. Learn methods to de-stress. Even something as simple as letting your shoulders drop when you know your stress is building. Open your palms and take deep breaths. Breathe in your for the count of 4 and then hold and breath out for the count of 5. Over the years we have learned a bad habit of not breathing deep enough. Our body needs our breath. The Hawaiian shamans would do the 'Ha' breath of life. They would breathe deeply in and when they breathe out they make the sound of 'Haaaaaaaaaaaa', until they feel they no longer need to breath out any further.

Exercise:

Do something to flow with the Universe at least once a week. A massage. A type of flowing dance, Tai Chi, Yoga, Massage, or go swimming. Just feel like your energy is flowing with the Universe.

Day 15

Day 15: laugh/comedy movies.

It is so important to have a sense of humour in life. Most people don't quite understand how important it is. Watch comedy movies. Have at least 1 good laugh every day. Try and see the funny side of each day and every situation.

Be around people that make you happy and bring your vibes up.

Exercise:

1. Make a list of your favourite comedy movies:

2. Here are a short list of some of mine that keep me laughing hysterically:

3. Meet the Fokkers

4. Oldschool

5. My cousin Vinny

6. Bridesmaids

7. Naked gun 2 ½

8. A fish called Wanda

9. Caddyshack

Obviously check the age ratings for each movie you chose to watch. There are also some great feelgood movies to make you feel great too. The Secret – Dare to Dream is one of my favourite feel good movies as well. So the first part of the exercise is to chose a good movie or comedy show to watch at lease 3 times a week. I would watch one once a day if you want to keep on a good vibe. Even just a comedy show/comedian or just a short sketch from a show. Always see the funny side of life too and joke around at the appropriate time as much as possible. Speak to friends who make you laugh as much as possible.

Go to a comedy show. Just see the funny side of life. If you really think about it you can turn most things around and see the funny side of life. Obviously when you need to be serious, you need to be serious but if you don't - be funny!

Day 16

Day 16: Affirmations/Learn to write your own affirmations.

So while you go through your day keep extra vigilant around your thoughts and make sure that they are mostly positive with positive vibes to go with it. I cant tell you how important this point is.

Be aware of your thoughts and words that you are using throughout the day. Not everyone can be positive 100% of the time but we need to realise what sort of impact our thoughts and words have on our day/vibes/manifestations.

Ask yourself questions about what you want in life and then put them into sentences. See how your body feels when you say them.

The key to affirmations is how you genuinely feel about them deep down. If your conscious and subconscious feel that you deserve and could receive what you are asking for it is more likely that you will get it. Otherwise you will get the thing you feel you 'don't deserve' and then you could lose it a week or so after manifesting it. For example if you want to win a million dollars but you feel 50 thousand is more believable and feels more realistic in yourself, then go ahead and manifest that 50 thousand and then work upwards to get your million.

The key to good affirmations is to also make them as exciting as possible. Sometimes changing all your usual affirmations into questions helps a lot.

Exercise:

1. Write your own affirmations. Use your goals and dreams as the subjects of your affirmations.

2. After writing your usual affirmations change them into questions and see how your body reacts and feels about each. If they feel more powerful that way. For example:

I am extremely happy.

Change to:

Why am I always so happy?

Day 17

Day 17: Using your senses to manifest.

I believe one of the reasons we have our senses is to help us manifest and stay in a wonderful happy vibe. You can change the way you feel just by using your senses.

Exercise:

1. Make sure that you always have lovely smells in your home/car etc. Incense or lovely essential oils in a diffuser. Lovely flowers in the home that give off a nice aroma. Nice cooking or fruit cakes that smell good. Good washing powders that make your clothes and bedclothes smell wonderful. Wear nice perfume.

2. Always have sounds around you that make you happy and inspire you. Either music that you enjoy or sounds you love like the sound of waves, the sound of a waterfall/river. Running water in the garden. Even silence if that is what you prefer and it makes you feel happy. Play happy music whenever you can.

3. Tastes: Cook food that not only smells good but tastes good as well. Do not eat bland foods.

4. Have fabrics around you that feel amazing. Lovely soft blankets, fleeces, wear clothes that feel good against your skin.

5. Touch: Remember to spend time with your animals stroking their beautiful soft fur. Enjoy their unconditional love that they are so happy to give you. Always wear fabrics that feel good. Have a couch or sofa that feels good. A carpet that feels good under your feet. A lovely blanket to wrap yourself in on a cold night. Nice bedclothes that feel great against your skin.

Day 18

Day 18: The Law of attraction, a Universal law

How the Law of attraction works:
The Law of Attraction works if you know how to use it. Knowing how the Law of Attraction works will help you with your entire life. What is the Law of Attraction? The Law of Attraction is a way of focusing on what you want in life and adding emotional charge to it. Imagining you already have it and then it has no choice but to manifest into your life. Ask,

believe, work and achieve. Also make sure to give off the right vibes. You need to be in the same vibration as what you would like to attract.

The Law of Attraction encourages you to ask for what you want and then let it go. Don't hold on too tightly and don't become desperate. That will only push away your manifestation. Once you have asked for it and used manifestation techniques you know that your manifestation is already there in the 'ethers' and it will manifest into your life at the right time and when you feel deep down that you deserve all the goodness that you want. The deserving feelings sometimes are hidden deep in your subconscious so as said above its good to use some meditations/hypnotherapy/affirmations to help you change your inner 'tapes' to re-write how your inner mind sees you.

And of course your feelings emotions and beliefs come into play with the Law of Attraction too.

The Law of Attraction is always: like attracts like. So if you are attracting things into your life that you don't like, look at what you are giving out. Life is like a mirror. We attract to us what we give out.

Remember there is always plenty of what you want in life. So never think in terms of lack. That will push your manifestation away. If its money you want imagine its flowing all around you. Dropping from the sky. Or the whole ocean is replaced with a sea of money that you can reach out and get whenever you want. Imagine too that there is a cash machine that gives out loads of money whenever you may need it. It will always be there for you without you even having to think about it. Its like air it will always be there, you will never be lacking in it.

Exercise:

Look around you and your life as it is at the moment and see how much of your life you have manifested. Even if its something you don't like or caused by what you think is other people. It could be an emotional thing but realise your emotions effect what you manifest into your life. Try and look for the things you wanted years ago and you didn't have and realise and celebrate what you have managed to manifest in your life. When you realise that you have already manifested things in your life that you wanted previously then you will realise if you want something enough you can manifest it. You are a manifestor you are a creator.

Day 19

Day 19: Law of Assumption

The Law of Assumption is a law that is not talked about a lot, but it was proposed by Neville Goddard in the early 19th Century, so it has been written about for much longer that we would expect. The Law of Assumption is even more powerful than the Law of attraction as it can work a lot faster. By expecting that the manifested outcome has already occurred and imagining it is happening right at this exact moment in time, living your life like it has already happened, it will have no choice but to come into your life. Walk around as if you are already in the house of your dreams, or you are in the country that you want to live in already. If you want to believe you have the job of your dreams, set an alarm to get up every morning. Dress in your best work clothes and imagine you have to job or go out and purchase clothes for your dream job. What you assume, you will get. But dont forget to take the steps and put the work in too.

Exercise:

1. Make assumptions at the beginning of you day as to how your day has gone.

2. Test out the Law of Assumption by assuming that you have something that you really want and live your life accordingly. See how what you want will appear in your life quicker that you expected.

3. Take the action steps as necessary.

Day 20

Day 20: Who are your Role models/Idols?

Realise you can have anything and everything that you want. Look at people who have achieved it from scratch: for example, Madonna, Richard Branson, Elon Musk etc. I am not promoting any of the above people but you cannot deny that these people have had a goal of one sort or another and achieved it. There are thousands if not millions more who have done similar. One of the most amazing thoughts in life is that your mind was given to you so that you can imagine and create anything and everything you want in life :) Yes, you are no different from anyone who has already achieved a lot in their lives.

Exercise:

1. Write down a list of your role models.

2. For each person that you feel is your role model, ask yourself these questions:

    i. How did they become successful?

    ii. What qualities did they possess that you could emulate?

    iii. How did they manifest their lives.....maybe read their autobiographies?

    iv. Did they have any setbacks but overcame them?

    v. Did they believe in themselves?

Day 21

Day 21: Love yourself/Increase your self esteem and your uniqueness & smile.

Exercise:

One of the best practices you can do every morning when you go in the bathroom or in from of a mirror is, look yourself in the eye and say "Thank you", "I love you", "you are beautiful", and mean it with all your heart. This is not a conceited love. Look after yourself. Always compliment yourself.

Love & blessings.

Exercise:

Bless & increase your blessings. While walking down the street if you see someone or something that has a quality that you would like bless that person or thing. If you see someone with a great body/figure for example, say to yourself "thank you for my wonderful and healthy, fit and sexy body". Find lots of things in your day to appreciate. The more you appreciate others, the more it will bless you.

Day 22

Day 22: Gratitude/Gratitude journal to do every day

This is one of the most magical practices you will ever do. I only started this practice later on in my spiritual journey. I was not aware how powerful it really was and how it could shift things very quickly for the positive in your life. It really is full of magic. The more grateful you are for what is already happening in your life the more will manifest. As if by magic showing your gratitude every day will automatically shift things for the positive for you without you even trying. It will change your life. One by one things will start coming into your life that you have always been hoping for. The more you are grateful for, the more you will receive into your life.

Exercise:

- Write down 100 things you are grateful for and read it out aloud to yourself.

- The more you are grateful for in every life area the more you will manifest.

- Before you go to sleep and when you wake up, think of at least 5 – 10 things that you are grateful for in your life.

- The Universe will bless you if it knows that you are already grateful for what you have.

Huna principles and how to use them:

The 7 Huna principles (Serge Kahili King)

Day 23

7 Huna Principles:

Day 23: . IKE: The world is what you think it is.

You are creating your world with every thought.

Have I dreamed the right life into reality? Look around and see if you are pleased with the dream of life you have created.

Is my 'world' based around the beliefs of others or my own beliefs and values?

Am I living the spiritual beliefs that are important to me or am I just going with what someone else has told me or am I still believing the religion I was brought up with and not questioning it at all?

Am I actually fearful of living the life of my dreams so I am still creating your 'comfort zone' reality?

Do you realise you can create a whole new reality and timeline for yourself?

Exercise:

Use a creative meditation to change or improve the outcome of a situation. For example if you are going into a meeting, imagine in every detail how the meeting will proceed. Athletes already use these techniques to win races etc. Starting by dreaming your life into being is the best way and the best foundation to starting and doing anything in life

Day 24

Day 24: KALA: There are no limits ... Freedom

The only limits there are, are the limits you put onto things yourself. Anything is possible.

As we are all connected as part of the Universe we can all influence each other and our physical world around us. Everything is connected.

Exercise:

Where are you putting limits on yourself?

Do you feel inadequate or not good enough?

Are you expecting life to be difficult?

Have an honest look at yourself and see if you are playing the victim in certain areas of your life?

Day 25

Day 25: MAKIA: Energy flows where attention goes.

The whole world is made purely of energy. We are all made up of energy, a Universal energy. Energy is either static or flowing. Chairs, tables, and solid structures are made of energy too but the density of their energies make them appear solid.

Energy can be changed by our focus on the energy. If you focus on something it brings our energy to it and affects the energy of what we are concentrating on. So always watch your thoughts and what you are concentrating on. And be careful what you wish for as you need to be prepared to get it.

You can change things by focusing on them. Watch what you focus on.

Exercise:

i. Watch what happens when you play a sport. If you put more attention on, for example the ball in golf whether it will move more towards where you would like it to go to. Focusing on something pushes it to where you would like to go. Try it …

ii. Try focusing on the clouds on a cloudy day. Imagine them dispersing and making a hole in the clouds to let out the sun……see what happens

Day 26

Day 26: MANAWA: Now is the moment of power.

You created where you are now in life. There is no such thing as time. Time is happening now. The power of living in the present is amazing. The present is all that there is. Because now is the only time. Now is the only time that has any power over you.

Realise you have to seize the moment and get the most out of every moment and every day of your life. Today and this hour/minute could be your last day so live each minute as if it could be your last, and if you think about things this way you will make the most of every moment of your life.

Exercise:

1. What can you do right now to improve your life or get to the goals you are working on?

2. How can you make the most of every day of your life?

3. How can you live in the moment?

Day 27

Day 27: ALOHA: To love is to be happy with.

Love is … to share affection and joy. Love exists to the degree you are happy with something. Love increases as judgement decreases. Everything is aware, alive & responsive and wants love. Everything needs love. Love is very important. Love is the greatest energy in the Universe.

Whatever you are happy with, you will love. Think about that statement. Sometimes it just takes a different way of looking at things or approaching things to make them a positive part of your life. Look for the good in everything and you will find the love.

Everything wants love. Such a true statement. Whatever you pour your love onto will improve. If its food, a room, another person, a pet. Everything can feel your love. Do everything with love and you will always get the best out of whatever you are putting your love into.

Exercise:

Try an experiment. Take a day (day 27) and use that day as an experiment. All day with everything you do and get up to put as much love as possible into everything you do and every one you come into contact with. Even if you don't like the person, try sending love to them and see how your relationship with them changes. Look for something good in them. Even if its just something very small like you like their hair colour or you like their shirt etc. Let me know how it goes :)

Day 28

Day 28: MANA: All power comes from within.

If we are brought up in a traditional religious environment then you may have been taught that all power is outside of ourselves but the Universal creation/creator power is also inside us. We can create whatever we want from inside of us. Our mind was created for us to be a creator on earth. We have the power of the Creator/Source within us. Realising you can create your own experiences from your own body, mind and spirit.

Everything you have created in life you've created from your own desires, beliefs, fears and expectations, conscious or unconscious. Very similar to the Law of Attraction and the Law of Assumption.

No one else can control your emotions either. You control how you feel about every situation and person in life. Just because they don't act the way you want them to does not mean you should feel that they are controlling your emotions. You are the one who can make the decision to be happy or sad, frustrated, angry, disappointed etc in the way a person is acting. They are not controlling the emotions going on in your head, you are. You have the power.

Exercise:

Look at how you look at situations and people in your life and in your day (day 28). Do you let them control you or do you have control over the way they or the situation effects you?

Day 29

Day 29: PONO: Effectiveness is the measure of truth.

If it works, it works. If it works, its Huna. It's like the old saying the proof of the pudding is in the eating.

What is really important is what works. It doesn't matter what belief system it comes from if it works it works. There is always another way of doing things. If you had a chronic illness you would try anything to help it. Always be flexible and don't only go with one belief system.

The end justifies the means. Whichever way you do something will determine the outcome. You have to work within the belief systems of others to help them. There is always, always another way to do something To get to the end result that you want.

Exercise:

Imagine a way you do something. Then imagine getting the same result by a different method. Effectiveness is the goal, not proving a belief system. There are always other ways of doing things. If one method doesn't work use another one.

Always test out theories. If you find it works it is true and it's therefore Huna.

Day 30

Day 30: How far have you come on your journey and do you need to add any more milestones?

How close are you to achieving your goal? If you are not there yet, keep practicing the Universal law & Huna principles and following your goals and your human needs and you will get there and be happy. Have a look at any steps you are struggling with and re-do them/it. Practice the steps until they become part of your subconscious. It's like riding a bike or driving a car at first - you really have to be mindful and concentrate, but after a while your autopilot and subconscious kick in and you are able to subconsciously be in any zone that you need to be in.

Mark your goals from 1 – 10 and compare it to how you felt about your goals in chapter 1 and celebrate every achievement!

Congratulations, you've done an amazing job!

Printed in Great Britain
by Amazon